# To God be the Glory

An inspiring testimony of living faith from two famous Christian personalities—Corrie Ten Boom and Billy Graham. Among topics covered from their writings are: Suffering, Facing Death, Comfort, Memories, Forgiveness, God's Presence, Prayer, Marriage, Sin, Broken Homes, Money, Despair and Mercy.

The reader will want to read and reread these deeply meaningful words.

TO GOD BE THE GLORY

# TO GOD BE THE GLORY

Edited by Roger Elwood

A testimony of living faith from two
famous Christian personalities:
CORRIE TEN BOOM and
BILLY GRAHAM

*Phoenix Press*

# WALKER AND COMPANY
*New York*

Large Print Edition published by arrangement with
Ideals Publishing Corp.

ACKNOWLEDGMENTS
Quotes in this book are from Corrie ten Boom, reprinted by permission of the Author and the Author's Agent, and are copyrighted as follows: 1954 A PRISONER, AND YET, Christian Literature Crusade, London; 1967 PLENTY FOR EVERYBODY, Christian Literature Crusade, London; 1969 MARCHING ORDERS FOR THE END BATTLE, Christian Literature Crusade, London; 1971 THE HIDING PLACE, Corrie ten Boom; 1974 TRAMP FOR THE LORD, Corrie ten Boom and Jamie Buckingham.

**Library of Congress Cataloging in Publication Data**

Main entry under title:

To God be the glory.

   1. Ten Boom, Corrie.   2. Graham, Billy, 1918–
3. Christian life—1960–    .  4. Large type books.
I. Ten Boom, Corrie.   II. Graham, Billy, 1918–
III. Elwood, Roger.
[BR1700.2.T6   1984]     242       84-16676
ISBN 0-8027-2473-6

This edition printed in 1986.

Printed in the United States of America

**First Large Print Edition, 1984**
**Walker and Company**
**720 Fifth Avenue**
**New York, New York 10019**

10  9  8  7  6  5  4  3  2

# Introduction

What we have put together in *To God Be the Glory* are quotes from Corrie ten Boom and Billy Graham dealing with subjects of abiding interest to most readers. In several instances, Ruth Graham is included, for you would have to search a long time in order to discover a union more firmly based on Christian marital principles—and you would have to search at least as hard to find a more devoted, happy couple.

Our sincere desire is that you will find this book to be of value to you at various moments in your life, and that some of the wisdom possessed by these two renowned Christians will help you in your own earthly walk.

*Roger Elwood*

*from the writings of*

# Corrie ten Boom

## Youthful Dreams

When I was about twelve, I decided that I wanted to be a writer. I curled up on my bed, pad of paper on my lap, and wove a wonderful fantasy about the adventures of Nollie, Josien, Dot, and all of Dot's brothers and sisters on a holiday without our parents. It was a beautiful story, filled with more adventure than Dickens, and more vivid character sketches than Louisa May Alcott. How famous I would be!

Betsie shattered my dreams. She came into the room and asked, "What's that?"

It seemed quite obvious to me. "It's a book I'm writing," I answered as smugly as a sister seven years younger could reply to the ridiculous question of a grown-up.

Betsie seldom voiced any words of discouragement, but this time she said, "How foolish . . . you can't write a book."

I just won't show anyone my book anymore, I thought. So I hid it in the attic and forgot the priceless manuscript for several months.

When I remembered later to take the papers out of their secret niche, there was only one-tenth of this potential best seller left. The rest was eaten by the mice. I was so disappointed that I decided never to write a book again.

## Spiritual Food

When the disciples were passing out the food to the five thousand, they must have rejoiced in their hearts, seeing the miracle —plenty for everyone. So when a Christian receives the happy Biblical messages, straight from the hands of Jesus, he too will experience—plenty for everyone.

An abundant richness of strength is at our disposal. We need this strength. Let us then be conscious of it in our way of living. This richness does not depend on circumstances. We must realize this fully, because circumstances will be difficult in the final battle. But we shall never lack anything.

## Suffering

When one does a lot of traveling, there is no time for sickness or accidents. Yet my prison experiences had affected my body and, too, I have been "a long time young." But the Lord restoreth my health and strength and daily I enjoy His constant care. He knows that it is difficult to work when one feels unwell and also that giving too much attention to little symptoms is playing into the hands of the enemy, who uses it to depress us until we see things out of all proportion to their true value. I will not say that every illness is out of the plan of God, for after all, we are training for higher service; and I know that suffering can be part of that training.

## Possession

In Germany, a well-known evangelist had a dreadful experience. A lady came to him in great agony. The expression of her eyes was terrible. The minister had the discernment to see that she was demon-possessed, and in his longing to help her, he laid his hands on her for healing. At the moment when he touched her, he fell backwards on the floor and was unconscious for a whole hour! After recovering, he found that the woman had drowned herself in the river!

When I asked him, "Did you not know that you may never touch a person who is demon-possessed?" he confessed that he had not known that it was dangerous.

Here was a man with a thorough theological training, much Bible knowledge, a heart full of love to help his people, but he failed for lack of knowledge.

Jesus said, "Cast out demons . . . lay hands on the sick" (Mark 16:17, 18). He did not say: "Lay hands on the demon-possessed."

. . . there was defeat that day! I never understood why! Was there perhaps anger or resentment in my heart? That could have been the reason! For if we give room to any sin, we ally ourselves with the enemy, and we stand powerless in the battle!

## Facing Death

The quiet years of the early 1920s in our

home were punctuated by the sound of Tante Anna's fading alto voice, singing the great old hymns of the church. As the once-vigorous body became weaker, she stayed in bed most of the time, memorizing verse after verse from her worn hymnal. She knew most of the songs slightly, but now learned all the words from the first to the last line. "I've never had time to memorize," she said, "and it's such a joy."

She knew that her time on earth was limited, but she seemed determined to enter heaven with a song on her lips.

When a day in the shop had been particularly difficult, or someone had come to the house burdened with heavy sorrow, it was an encouragement to hear from the little bedroom upstairs the beautiful words:

He leadeth me, Oh! blessed thought!
O words with heavenly comfort fraught!
Whate'er I do, where'er I be,
Still 'tis God's hand that leadeth me.

After a short, severe illness, God led Tante Anna to her new home in heaven. Father, Betsie, and I sat at the big oval table, once so crowded with all the ten Booms, and talked about the past.

"It's a new life now, Corrie; we must remember the past, but live in anticipation of the future."

## Comfort

Outside, the sun was shining. A bird was softly singing a song of spring. Through the twenty-eight rectangles of my window I could see gold-tipped even clouds. And my fancy took flight. I saw the wide sea, the white-capped waves. I actually heard the murmur of the sea, for the west wind was blowing. I was alone within the close confines of my cell, but outside of my cell was the great prison, and outside of that the great wide world, where birds fly and the sea murmurs. And in that world were people who were thinking about us.

A Red Cross parcel was lying just outside my door. It represented contact with those friendly people who would, perhaps, come very soon to set us free. All the prisoners took courage when the Red Cross parcels arrived on alternate Wednesdays.

The door opened just as I was trying to

stand on my trembling legs.

"Come and fetch it yourself; you're walking anyway. I shall not bring it to you." How painful indifference can be!

I unpacked the parcel. It was filled with delicious, tasty things, selected by understanding people who knew what was good for us. Would this, perhaps, be my last parcel? Should we, perhaps, be free in a week or two?

Biscuits, a croquette, caramels. But why did I take no delight in these things? There was really no pleasure in nibbling at this or that dainty by myself. It occurred to me to offer some to the *Wachtmeisterin*, but I let the impulse pass.

I knew I should never in the future (was there to be a future?) eat dainties by myself. If I ever had anything good to eat, I should remember cell 384 and invite others to enjoy it with me.

It was dark in my cell.

I talked with my Saviour. Never before had fellowship with Him been so close. It was a joy I hoped would continue unchanged. I was a prisoner—and yet . . . how free!

## Vows

To be a conqueror it is very important to remain faithful. It is good to ask yourself: "Did I ever vow to God, and then not keep it?" Have you ever been singing with your whole heart after an inspiring talk: "Take my life and let it be consecrated, Lord, to Thee. Take my silver and my gold; take my moments and my days . . ."?

## Temptations

Restore unto me the joy of thy salvation (Ps. 51:12).

In an American university I spoke with a girl whose problem was temptations. "I doubt," she said, "whether I am a Christian. I did make a decision for Christ and trusted Him as my Saviour but I am so often filled with temptations—terrible thoughts enter into my head and my heart—that I fear I am not a Christian at all."

"Temptation is no sin," I replied. "Jesus was tempted. As a great preacher once said, 'You cannot stop birds from flying over your head, but you can prevent them from building a nest in your hair.' The Lord Jesus gives the strength needed in order that we may not yield to temptation. What about your parents? Are you still their daughter, even when you sin?"

"Yes, I am: but a naughty one."

"That is so. A sinning child of God is still a child of God, but a disobedient one."

"But I have lost my joy."

"That is because sin causes us to lose our fellowship. Your relationship with Him is just the same. Jesus will be your Victor. He died for you and now He lives for you."

Living, He loved me;
Dying, He saved me;
Buried, He carried my sins far away;
Rising, He justified freely forever;
One day He's coming—O glorious day!

Forgiveness is the key which unlocks the door of resentment and the handcuffs of hatred. It breaks the chains of bitterness and the shackles of selfishness. The forgiveness of Jesus not only takes away our sins, but it also makes them as if they had never been.

# Memories

In the Kenaupark of Haarlem stood a beautiful tree, a wild cherry. Every spring it bore such a wealth of blossoms that the residents of Haarlem called it "the bride of Haarlem." If one stood under it and looked up he would see a luxuriant canopy of white blossoms. Father would go to see it each spring. Betsie and I would watch the blossoms grow larger and larger, and stand under the tree, arm in arm, when the beauty was at its height. Then for days our morning walk would take us over the carpet of fallen petals.

Now "the bride of Haarlem" had been chopped down. The massive trunk had not been too much for even unskilled hands to lay low in time of need. The people of Haarlem had no fuel with which to cook their scanty rations, and in their cold and hunger they did not think of spring beauty or of tradition.

I walked through the Kenaupark, looking for the tree. But it was gone! And I was walking alone. Betsie, my sister, whom Haarlem had loved, was not at my side.

10

Truly, "the bride of Haarlem" had been cut down. Nor was my father's arm linked in mine, for "Haarlem's Grand Old Man" had died in a cruel prison.

I looked up. April clouds obscured the sun; but they themselves were radiant with a golden luster that shed a glow over the earth and touched everything with color.

Clouds, too, can give light if only the sun shines on them.

Every Christian is called to be on duty twenty-four hours every day in 'the King's business'. Your office, your school, your kitchen, your drawing-room, your factory, all are a mission field. Jesus still says, 'Give the hungry to eat'.

The name that is above every name in heaven or on earth is the name: Jesus, Saviour! He is our strength . . . That name brings heaven and earth together. One cannot overestimate the value of that name in the great final battle.

## Satan's Attack

Another form of attack that Satan uses is to

bring to the memory of the young convert the weaknesses and sins of the past and then suggest that because of them he can never be called a faithful follower of Christ. No amount of reasoning or argument can overcome this temptation but only the Word of God, which says in 1 Corinthians 10:13, "There hath no temptation taken you but such as is common to man: but God is faithful, who will not suffer you to be tempted above that ye are able; but will with the temptation also make a way of escape, that ye may be able to bear it."

Bringing the Gospel to subnormal people is not popular work in the eyes of the world. To convert a "big shot" is more important than to change a subnormal person who cannot organize a mission, cannot start a drive to collect money, cannot write books, and cannot do what splendid, gifted Christians can.

Does heaven have the same standards as on earth? I do not think so.

I know that the last words of Jesus, before going to heaven, were, "Go ye—and preach the Gospel to every creature." And I think

12

that the subnormal have received a special grace to enable them to understand the Gospel.

Have you given God His money's worth? He paid a high price for you.

Then Holland surrendered. I walked in the street with Father, and everyone was talking to everyone else. In that moment there was a oneness which I had never seen before. We were together in the great suffering, humiliation, and defeat of our nation. Although my heart was aching with misery, there was encouragement that people could be so united.

In the millennium we will be like that. The whole world will be covered with the knowledge of God like the waters cover the bottom of the sea. The oneness will not be misery, but in our communion with the Lord.

## Teammates

Working in Germany is a delight. The ministers and I get along well, working, praying and striving together. A team traveling with me would be ideal, but since that is not yet possible, God has given me as teammates the ministers in whose churches I work. Though differing in background and training, our common aim unites us: the winning of souls for eternity, and helping the children of God to learn that "Jesus is Victor."

It was such a joy to know that the Holy Spirit doesn't need a high IQ in a person to reveal Himself. Even people of normal or superior intelligence need the Lord to understand the spiritual truths which are only spiritually discerned.

"When you belong to the Lord, there's not one single thing you have to conquer in your own strength. The hairs of your head are numbered; can anything be more trivial than that?"

When the marching orders of our King are given and seem very exacting, then we need not fear, for He Himself gives us the courage, the faithfulness, and the strength to obey Him.

Our faithfulness to God is the fruit of the Spirit. That becomes a quality in us only when we give room to the Holy Spirit in our hearts and lives. Be filled with God's Spirit, and faithfulness, the fruit of the Spirit, will be your portion.

## Victorious Living

When the devil cannot keep us back, he tries to push us so fast that we exaggerate. Then we are in danger of forgetting to love. It is very important for us to understand that all these temptations and trials belong to training for the final battle. The "trainer," the Holy Spirit, gives us what we need. He teaches us to be patient, to look at the Lord, to pay attention to our fellow warriors, and not to burden ourselves with superfluous luggage. This all is a part of the victorious life; while He trains conquerors, He comforts us with His bountiful promises.

It is so important to know that in the final battle the joy of the Holy Spirit is available for us in all circumstances.

When someone dies, people are confronted with eternity, and there is the right opportunity to speak about the security of eternal life that only Jesus can give.

To be hid with Christ in God. What a comfort to know that we belong to the victorious army of God, when we look at the seemingly superior forces of the enemy.

Children need the wisdom of their elders; the aging need the encouragement of a child's exuberance.

. . . I have seen that God can use "good" and "bad" people. I know many evangelists who are still serving their time in prison. What God can do with a murderer who surrenders fully to Him! Fellows, there is also hope for us.

## Forgiveness

When we forgive others we often bury the hatchet, leaving the handle out: ready for future use. God does not. He blots out our sins like a cloud; you never see a cloud again once it has evaporated. We are on the Lord's side and thus are yoke-fellows with Jesus, so we can face the foe, being more than conquerors through Him who loves us. Do not ask:

"Can I be kept from sinning if I keep close to Him?" But rather:

"Can I be kept from sinning if He keeps close to me?"

You will see what a joy it is to surrender to Jesus. He will go with you to the point where you went astray and change the whole situation with His presence.

When we pray, it doesn't matter whether it is a beautiful prayer or a prayer from our prayer book, or perhaps just a cry of distress directly to the Lord.

"I experienced the miracle that the highest potential of God's love and power is available to us in the trivial things of everyday life."

If you must tell something negative about someone else, first tell ten positive qualities about him.

As the end times draw closer and closer, so does the power of God grow greater and greater.

When we were alone, I let them talk and talk about their aunt. I have found this is one of the most important things to do for a person who is grieving—have him talk about the loved one who is gone.

Connected with Him in His love, I am more than conqueror; without Him, I am nothing. Like some railway tickets in America, I am "Not good if detached."

## Unclaimed Deposits

The story goes that in a Scottish bank there were forty million pounds in unclaimed deposits! How many unclaimed deposits there are in the Bible! Are we professors or possessors? Remember that every promise of God is backed by the golden reserves of the bank of heaven, available to us here and now, in good times or bad. When the worst happens, yet the best remains. Or as another has remarked, the Christian life is a walk into a splendid palace through marvelous antechambers. We cannot go into the second room if we have not passed through the first; we cannot reach the fifth if we are not willing to enter the fourth.

It never ceases to amaze me the way the Lord creates a bond among believers which reaches across continents, beyond race and color. This spiritual bond is something man has tried to establish with big national or world councils and organized ecumenical movements, but always misses when the Spirit of the Lord is not present.

. . . all we do through our own strength has to be cleansed, but what we do through the Lord has value for time and eternity . . . What challenges we have today! I remember what Father often said: "When Jesus takes your hand He keeps you tight. When Jesus keeps you tight He leads you through life. When Jesus leads you through life He brings you safely home."

I do not believe immediately in telling new Christians what they should and should not do: such things can be left safely to the Holy

Spirit. For, after all, we do not bring people to a faith, a religion, or a doctrine, but to a person, Jesus Christ.

## Man's Art

Betsie could turn a drab room into a place of charm; she could transform a dull happening into a rollicking, amusing story. We were introduced to art at an early age, and Betsie could make an art exhibit a tremendous treat when she was the guide.

We were so rich in art in Holland, and very conscious of our heritage from the masters of the past. When Betsie took me to the Frans Hals museum in Haarlem, she would point out the beauty of each masterpiece.

"Look, Corrie, at the way Hals paints the faces of his subjects. Aren't they marvelous? And look at their hands—have you ever seen anything more beautiful?"

She would explain to me the exceptional talents of Rembrandt, showing me how he expressed the character of those he painted. Betsie could weave stories through a visit to an art exhibit in such an exciting way that I couldn't wait for the next chapter. It added to the richness of my childhood and the quality of my appreciation for classical art and music.

Conversion is to turn about: 180 degrees. The original attitude of man is that he lives away from God. After conversion you live with your face towards God.

## The Feebleminded

Once, in a concentration camp, I was questioned by a Nazi officer. He asked me much about my life, about my work in the Underground, and about my spare time. I told him that I had given Bible lessons to subnormal people.

"Don't you regard that as a waste of time?" he asked. "Surely it is much better to convert a normal person than a subnormal one."

This was fully in accord with his Nazi way of thinking. So I told him about Jesus, who had always cared for all who were weak and despised, adding that it might well be possible that the officer and I were much less important in the sight of the Lord Jesus than one of these poor creatures. I was sent back to my cell.

The next morning the officer sent for me and said that he had slept badly. He had thought much about what I had said.

"You spoke about Jesus," he said. "I don't know anything about Him. Tell me what you know of Him."

I then spoke of the Lord Jesus as the Light of the World who can lighten our life, if we give ourselves to Him and receive Him as our Saviour and Lord. Three days I was questioned and three days I had the opportunity to speak about the Gospel of Jesus Christ.

A conversation about the feebleminded had changed a most dangerous moment for a prisoner into a testimony to the glory of God.

Once a feebleminded girl answered a question of mine which might have baffled a person of normal intelligence. I asked, "What is a prophet and what is a priest?"

She said, "They are both messengers between God and man."

I continued, "Then they are the same—a prophet and a priest?"

She thought a while and then answered.

"No, a prophet has his back to God and his face to us—and a priest has his face to God and his back to us."

## Demonic Opposition

Opposition to lives which are yielded to Jesus Christ takes many forms, some dramatic, some subtle. Satan is a clever angel of light, but sometimes he chooses supernatural ways to frighten us into inactivity.

During a time at camp with the girls, I was singing outside of the cabin after lights-out. The song had the words: "Don't be afraid for whatever is coming, your heavenly Father takes care of you."

Suddenly I heard horrible noises around me. It seemed as if among the trees some sort of beings were trying to make me stop. The noises grew and subsided, sending shivers through my body with their weird tones. While I sang, I pleaded with the Lord: "Cover me and protect me with Your blood, Lord Jesus . . . give me the strength to go on singing and speak through me to reach all these girls."

The noises remained and got louder and

23

more ugly, but I didn't stop. I knew that I stood on the front line of battle, but through Jesus, it was victory ground, not defeat or retreat. As soon as I had finished the song, the noises stopped, just as abruptly as they began.

I went to bed and thanked the Lord for His victory. The next morning I asked the girls if they had heard anything unusual the previous night. They answered that they had never heard me sing so beautifully. Nobody heard anything else.

It is not safe to pilot on feelings. My Bible is my instrument; flying on the Bible's instructions, acting on its readings, my plane keeps a straight course. If I pilot on my feelings, I could make dangerous mistakes.

We are in training for that great future, but this training period can be a victorious one only when we realize that we can and must surrender ourselves to the Lord Jesus. Live as rich as you are; cash your checks in the Bible; realize that you are what you are in Jesus Christ. The devil says that the bank account of the Bible is frozen by your sins. He is a liar. The bank account is full of the precious reserves of heaven's plenty. Surrender your past, present and future. Your past is a cancelled check; your present is cash; your future is a promissory note. Jesus bore your sins on the Cross: all was done and finished at Calvary. Now He lives for us.

Faith works to protect us against the fiery arrows of the enemy.

## God's Presence

The presence of the Lord is our great comfort. With Jesus hidden in God. He invites us: "Abide in me, and I in you." Be strong against a world of unbelief, without being ashamed for your King. We must be spirit-filled soldiers and must fight to gain the victory, until Jesus comes. He is our strength now, and also in the last battle.

There is fear in the heart of a disobedient servant when the master returns, but there is joy in the heart of an obedient child when the father comes home. How I should love it if Jesus should come today. Just imagine how wonderful it would be not to have to be sick, to die or to pass through the valley of the shadow of death.

## Prayer

If you will work for God, form a committee.
If you will work with God, form a prayer group.

During my trip from Formosa to Australia, I am able to stay for five days in Hong Kong. This beautiful island has riches and poverty side by side. It has the most beautiful window displays in the world, but also many slums full of refugees. It is a piece of free China with huge problems.

My time there is full of activity. I am in contact with many consecrated Christians. The meetings are extremely well organized, every minute of the day being put to good use.

One evening the Holy Spirit is obviously working in a group of young Christians who some time ago accepted Jesus Christ as their Saviour. On this particular evening they come to a full surrender and accept Him as their Victor. "Thanks be to God, which giveth us the victory through our Lord Jesus Christ" (1 Cor. 15:57).

One asks, "What is expected of us now?"

"The Lord will show you. Wait patiently for His guidance. But there is one thing I can advise you to do now, and that is to organize prayer cells. Prayer is not a prefix or a suffix; it is central. Over the whole world I see that God gives His children prayer cells. It is not only the Communists who form cells, but wherever two or three come together in Jesus's name, there is a cell for Him. In eternity we shall see how important prayer meetings have been."

A group of students in Chicago prayed every week for a number of unsaved fellow students. Eventually, everyone on the list was saved. One of them was Dr. Torrey Johnson, the founder of Youth for Christ. Wherever I have traveled over the world I have seen how this work has been blessed. Thousands and tens of thousands have found their Saviour through it. What was the first cause? Torrey Johnson? No; the prayers of those young men in Chicago. Intercession is so tremendously important that in Isaiah 59:16 is written, "God wondered that there was no intercessor."

"If you will work for God, form a committee. If you will work with God, form a prayer group."

That evening, we make plans for a weekly prayer meeting, and later I hear that more have commenced. The greatest thing we can do for one another is to pray. Prayer is striking the winning blow at the concealed enemy—our service is gathering up the results.

*from the writings of*

# Billy Graham

Perhaps you say, "But I don't know what to say when I pray." God does not mind your stumbling and halting phrases. He is not interested in your grammar. He is interested in your heart. I have a little boy only two years old. He stumbles and falters trying to express himself to me; but I think I love his little words that I cannot understand even more than I will appreciate his correct grammatical sentences when he grows older.

## Marriage

Never abandon hope for the salvation of that husband or wife, for the happiness of your home and the peace of mind you need are involved in his or her salvation. With two lives yielded to Jesus Christ, you will have the assurance of a God-planned home and of a life that is not only happy but blessed of God in a fruitful witness to Christ.

29

One thing the Bible does *not* teach is that sex in itself is sin. Far from being prudish, the Bible celebrates sex and its proper use, presenting it as God-created, God-ordained, God-blessed. It makes plain that God himself implanted the physical magnetism between the sexes for two reasons: for the propagation of the human race, and for the expression of that kind of love between man and wife that makes for true oneness. His command to the first man and woman to be "one flesh" was as important as His command to "be fruitful and multiply."

Shining through the Bible is God's readiness to forgive sin, sexual or otherwise, and His eagerness to bring peace of mind and heart to the repentant. But the natural consequences of our sins will have to be suffered. The ugly memories cannot be forgotten: the illegitimate baby cannot be unborn. David was forgiven his adultery, but he had to take his punishment.

## Women

I do not think that the Bible in any way teaches that women are inferior. The

Apostle Paul made a statement about women to the effect that they should be quiet. I believe the reason he said it was because in the synagogues of that day, women would sit in the balcony—as in some parts of the world today, and would talk so loudly that the rest of the people could not hear the speaker. So Paul said, let the women be quiet. That did not mean they were inferior.

It's a strange thing about this Book [Bible]. There are many things in it I don't understand and can't explain. Some of the questions I have about it I am sure will never be answered this side of Heaven. But I know one thing: it contains a mysterious power to direct all kinds and conditions of people into changed lives, and it helps to keep them changed. Inside these covers, on these printed pages, are the guides and signposts to the answers to all man's deepest needs. That is why I can open this Book before an audience of people and say, "This is the Word of God."

I can't turn the press off like a film star. I'm a clergyman. I must be available, responsive.

# Future

The Christian believes in a fabulous future, even though the present structure of modern society should disappear and all its progress should be wiped out by self-destruction as a result of man's failure. There is a sense in which the Kingdom of God is already here in the living presence of Christ in the hearts of all true believers. There is also, however, the ultimate consummation of all things, which is called the Kingdom of God. This is the fabulous future!

A problem I face in golf, is keeping my eye on the ball. That is a rule in every sport, whether it's baseball, football . . . golf. The New Testament speaks of "looking unto Jesus, the author and finisher of our faith" . . . It is thrilling to look to Jesus.

# Ambition

Ambition is an essential part of character, but it must be fixed on lawful objects and exercised in proper proportion.

Learn the secret of prayer. Christ's prayer life was one of the most amazing and impressive features of His earthly ministry. He prayed with His disciples. He prayed in secret. Sometimes He spent all night in prayer. If He, the sinless Son of God, could not live His earthly life without constant fellowship with God, can you?

We need to be reminded that there is nothing morbid about honestly confronting the fact of life's end, and preparing for it so that we may go gracefully and peacefully. St. Francis tried to live in such a way that when his time came to die he had nothing to get ready for. It was the Psalmist, one of the world's wisest men, who prayed, "So teach us to number our days, that we may apply our hearts unto wisdom." The fact is, we cannot truly face life until we have learned to face the fact that it will be taken away from us. Man's attitude toward this certainty shapes his deepest views of life.

## Sin

What is sin? Sin is transgression, lawbreaking, coming short of God's standards. You break a law of the United States and you are a lawbreaker. You break the moral law of God and you are a lawbreaker. Every man who has ever lived is a lawbreaker; he is a sinner in God's sight.

A few years ago I was invited to the home of one of the world's wealthiest men. The invitation seemed urgent, but I was scarcely prepared for the depths of my host's anxiety. Immediately after dinner, he drew me aside to say: "While I am now in good health, my age tells me that I haven't long to live. I've never thought much about death before, —but now I find my mind preoccupied with it, and the idea frightens me. I need help!"

Some of the radical groups in the country are being led by so-called clergymen. Where many of these men get the "reverend" in front of their names, I do not know. Certainly they don't get it from God.

## Emptiness

America is said to have the highest per capita

boredom of any spot on earth! We know that because we have the greatest variety and greatest number of artificial amusements of any country. People have become so empty that they can't even entertain themselves. They have to pay other people to amuse them, to make them laugh, to try to make them feel warm and happy and comfortable for a few minutes, to try to lose that awful, frightening, hollow feeling—that terrible, dreaded feeling of being lost and alone.

I don't think we can ever solve the race problem apart from the renewal of the human heart. I used to think we could. I remember the night they passed the '64 civil-rights bill. Hubert Humphrey came over to the White House, where I was a guest. He came straight over to me, and he said, "Billy, we've done it." But he said, "Now it's up to you and people like you because legislation alone is not going to solve these problems." And I've lived to see that Hubert Humphrey's prediction is correct.

I believe in the resurrection of the body, and I have in mind that in heaven we will look like what we were at our best on the earth.

Taking your children to church is futile unless you go with them. Reading the Bible is useless unless you as parents practice the precepts therein before your children. The best way to teach is by example, and children see what you believe better than they hear what you say.

The old saying goes, "Honesty is the best policy." But it is more than a policy that may be just an expediency. Honesty is a rewarding practice in peace of mind and heart, and it is often more difficult to be honest than to be dishonest.

## Broken Homes

Thousands of homes are almost on the rocks. Many couples are fearful lest their home, too, will be broken some day. There is one great insurance policy that you can take out in order to guarantee the unity and happiness of your home. It is simple: *Make Christ the center of your home.*

God could have just come and patted man on the back and said, "You're forgiven, so be reconciled." But then God would not have been just, and God is primarily and basically a God of justice and holiness. He would have been a liar. He said, "If you break My law, you'll die." Man had to die. So death came upon the world—physical death, spiritual death, eternal death.

We should work for peace but all we can really do is patch things up, because the real war is in man's own heart. Only when Christ comes again will the lion lie down with the lamb and the little white children of Alabama walk hand in hand with the little black children.

## Money, Power, Fame

Rudyard Kipling, speaking to a graduating class at McGill University, advised the graduates not to care too much for money, power or fame. He said: "Someday you will meet a man of such stature that he will care for none of these things . . . and then you will realize how poor you are."

Teach your children that honesty is akin to

happiness and that a good conscience is a valuable possession. Don't overload your teaching with "Don't do this," and "Don't do that," but make it positive, like the Bible, which says: "This do and thou shalt live."

No friend or anything shall ever come first in my life. I have resolved that the Lord Jesus Christ shall have all of me. I care not what the future holds. I have determined to follow Him at any cost.

Have a time to pray each day. Make it a habit—vital and necessary as your daily food. Learn to "pray without ceasing"—that is, live through the day breathing a prayer to God!

## Perfect Justice

Love and mercy have no stability without agreement on basic justice and fair play. Mercy always infers that justice and goodness are to be expected. Lowering the standards of justice is never to be a substitute for the concept of mercy.

If I am kidnapped by radicals or terrorists, don't try to ransom me—don't try to save my life. Let them kill me or do to me whatever they want to because I know I'm going to Heaven anyway. Don't give in to them. Don't negotiate. I don't believe that we ought to give in to kidnappers. People should not be allowed to preach or teach the violent overthrow of the American government. It's subversive. I am not afraid of threats—or death. We've had two incidents in five days involving people down from northern cities who were looking for me. Somehow the police learned of their plans —perhaps through informants—and the persons involved were detained before they could reach the Montreat area.

## The Brevity of Life

The Bible has much to say about the brevity of life and the necessity of preparing for eternity. We need a new awareness of the fact that death is rapidly approaching for all of us, and that the Bible has many warnings for us to prepare to meet God.

# Discipline

We are living in a day when many psychiatrists are saying that the child should be allowed to express himself freely and to do as he pleases. But the Bible teaches that there should be loving obedience on the part of the child; and that if he does not obey, then discipline should be exercised by the parents.

I remember in *The Shoes of the Fisherman* the cardinal who was taking care of the pope told him, "The longer you're in that office, the office of pope, the lonelier that chair will get." There is a loneliness to it. There are very few people that I can really open to and share my total heart with who wouldn't go out and tell it. I have people sharing their problems all day long, but I, too have problems, and I have to keep my own counsel. I can only share them, really, in the privacy of my room with God and with my wife.

# Prayer

In this modern age in which we live, we have learned to harness the power of the atom, but very few of us have learned how to develop fully the power of prayer. We have not yet learned that a man is more powerful on his knees than behind the most powerful weapons that can be developed.

If anything bothers me, it is the thought that at Judgment Day I may find that I have not been as faithful as some other minister who is slugging it out day after day with few visible achievements in a storefront in Harlem.

I believe that there's a gift that God has given me in asking people to come forward and make a commitment to Christ at the end of my sermons. And in the 5 minutes, or the 10 minutes, that this appeal lasts, when I'm standing there, not saying a word, it's when most of my strength leaves me. I cannot explain that. I don't usually get tired quickly. But I get tired in the invitation. This is when I become exhausted. I don't know what it is, but something is going out at the moment.

## Anxiety

Modern anxiety is not directed toward the real, valid, justified fears such as eternity, death and the judgment of God. This generation is dying, not from external pressure, but from internal combustion.

## The New Birth

As I interview many distressed, confused and frustrated Americans every week, I find that there is a growing consciousness of the need of a new birth or a new awakening in the order of things. As one young man poured out his heart in frank confession of his many failures to make a success of his life, he threw up his hands in resignation. Amidst penitent tears he said, "I guess I was just born wrong."

He was much nearer the center of Bible truth than he realized; for the Bible plainly indicated that not only he but *all*—rich, poor, high, low, servant and master, capitalist and laborer, kings and commoners— were born wrong. The Bible says, "For all have sinned, and come short of the glory of God" (Rom. 3:23).

I don't know what the future holds, but I know Who holds the future.

## Mercy

Jesus stopped dying on the cross long enough to answer the prayer of a thief. He stopped in a big crowd one day because someone touched the hem of His garment; and He'll stop to touch your life and change you, and forgive you. He knows you by name. He has the hairs of your head numbered. He has your name written in His books and everything that you have done from the time you were born to this hour. All the secret things, all the private things, they are all there. He knows all about you and He loves you. He says He'll forgive you if you will put your trust and your confidence in Him.

## Crisis

Ours is not a crisis limited to the political arena. It reaches down to private life and into every home. It goes from your home and mine to the White House as well. We are uncertain about our values and the true meaning of life. This is why atheistic existentialism has gained so many converts. True religion, which used to supply us with our value system, has shriveled—even as secularism has grown and threatens to engulf us completely. Our standards have eroded to a point where the phony and the counterfeit are the order of the day. Television, magazines, newspapers and advertising have created a culture in which nobody expects to say, or listen to, or hear the truth.

Every time I see my name up in lights, it makes me sick at heart, for God said He will share His glory with no man.

## Despair

There are some who are in deep despair. I receive many letters daily from people who are discouraged, depressed and ready to give up. They are yielding to the pessimism of our times, to the mood and spirit of our day. A man in England wrote, "It's too late to do anything about the world."

That isn't true. All is *not* lost. We still have the Bible, and ". . . the word of God is not bound" (2 Tim. 2:9). We still have the Holy Spirit. We still have the fellowship of believers. We still have the prayers of God's people. We still have an open door to most of the world for proclaiming the Gospel.

## Sacrifice

Christ will never ask you to give up something unless He gives you something better in exchange. He asked Peter to give up his nets, but He gave him "keys of heaven." He asked the little lad to give up his loaves and fishes, but He gave him a square meal. He asked the disciples to deny themselves, but He gave them life eternal.

## Faith

I heard of an incident that took place in Niagara Falls. A crowd watched as a man rolled a wheelbarrow filled with two hundred pounds of dirt back and forth on a tightrope across the falls. When he asked,

"How many of you believe I can roll a man across?" One spectator very excitedly shouted, "I know you can do it!" He said, "All right, brother, you're first!"

Historians will probably call our era "the age of anxiety." Though we have less to worry about than previous generations, we have more worry.

## Adultery

Real marriage, which is the foundation of the home, means the total commitment of husband and wife to each other and does not permit extra-marital adultery or any form of infidelity.

## Smoking

There is good reason why Christians speak out against the use of tobacco. The Bible teaches that when a man is converted to Christ and receives pardon for his sin, Christ enters into his heart to dwell. Having come to dwell, we are then to regard the human body as sacred. "Your body is a temple of the Holy Spirit which is in you, which you have from God, and ye are not your own. For ye were bought with a price; glorify God therefore in your body." And smoking is, quite obviously, detrimental to the temple of the body.

## Despondency

Christ can take discouragement and despondency out of your life. He can put a spring in your step and give you a thrill in your heart and a purpose in your mind. Optimism and cheerfulness are products of knowing Christ.

A child, like an adult, is inclined to follow the line of least resistance. Lying, theft and cheating are attempts to find the easiest way out of a situation. Teach your children that life isn't easy—that it is a struggle, a conflict, and that it takes more strength of character to do right than wrong.

## Belief

When we speak of Christian faith, we refer to certain beliefs and doctrines. These are of great importance, for Christian living presupposes Christian conviction. But it is possible to have beliefs which do not find expression in conduct. This belief of the head is often confused with real faith. The simple truth is: one really believes only that which he acts upon.

## Money

Think of the things that cannot be bought with money. It cannot buy health, friends, love, or peace of mind and heart. It cannot buy peace of soul. We come to the conclusion then, that money in itself is not worthy of the importance most people place upon it.

## Love

I don't believe a man and a woman can really love each other outside of Christ. I believe that Christ gives a new depth—to married love. A new dimension of love. He can rekindle the love of your heart.

## Crisis

If you are not strengthening the inner man by daily walking with God now, when a crisis comes you will quake with fear and give in, having no strength to stand up for Christ.

## Doubt

Doubt is the disease of this inquisitive, restless age. It is the price we pay for our advanced intelligence and civilization—the dim night of our resplendent day. But as the most beautiful light is born of darkness, so the faith that springs from conflict is often the strongest and the best.

# Large Print Inspirational Books from Walker

Would you like to be on our Large Print mailing list? Please send your name and address to:

B. Walker
Walker and Company
720 Fifth Avenue
New York, NY 10019

## A Book of Hours

Elizabeth Yates

## The Alphabet of Grace

Frederick Buechner

## The Adventure of Spiritual Healing

Michael Drury

## A Certain Life: Contemporary Meditations on the Way of Christ

Herbert O'Driscoll

## A Gathering of Hope

Helen Hayes

**Getting Through the Night:** Finding Your Way After the Loss of a Loved One

Eugenia Price

**Inner Healing:** God's Great Assurance

Theodore Dobson

**Instrument of Thy Peace**

Alan Paton

**The Irrational Season**

Madeleine L'Engle

**Jonathan Livingston Seagull**

Richard Bach

**Living Simply Through the Day**

Tilden Edwards

**The Power of Positive Thinking**

Norman Vincent Peale

**The Touch of the Earth**

Jean Hersey

**Gift From the Sea**
Anne Morrow Lindbergh

**A Grief Observed**
C.S. Lewis

**A Guide to Christian Meditation**
Marilyn Morgan Helleberg

**Up From Grief**
Bernardine Kreis and Alice Pattie

**Walking With Loneliness**
Paula Ripple

**The Way of the Wolf**
Martin Bell

**Who Will Deliver Us?**
Paul Zahl

**With Open Hands**
Henri Nouwen

action. . . . I don't know how to thank you, Superintendent. . . ."

The poor fellow seemed to be swimming around in the room, as if it had suddenly become too large for him, like an article of clothing that has stretched and engulfs the wearer. He looked at the bottle of Armagnac, almost poured himself a glass, but a sense of decorum held him back, and finally Maigret had to do it for him. He helped himself to a glass at the same time.

"Here's to your daughter and the end of all these misunderstandings."

Naud looked at him in wide-eyed astonishment. "Misunderstandings" was the very last word he had expected to hear.

"We have been chatting while you were upstairs. . . . I think your friend Groult has something very important to say to you. . . . Believe it or not, he is in the process of getting a divorce, though he hasn't told a soul. . . ."

Naud looked more and more at sea.

"Yes . . . And he has other plans. . . . All this probably won't make you jump for joy. . . . A cracked pot will never be the same as a perfect one, but it's still a pot. . . . Didn't someone mention that there is a morning train?"

"It leaves at 6:11," said Cavre. "And I think I'll take it."

"We'll travel together, then. . . . In the meantime, I am going to try to snatch a few hours' sleep."

He could not help saying to Alban as he went out:

"What a dirty trick!"

It was still foggy. Maigret refused point-blank to let anyone take him to the station, and Etienne Naud bowed before his wish.

"I don't know how to thank you, Superintendent. I didn't behave toward you as I should have. . . ."

"You have treated me extremely well, and I've shared some excellent meals with you."

"Will you tell my brother-in-law . . ."

"Of course I will! Oh! One piece of advice, if I may be so bold . . . Don't be too hard on your daughter."

A pathetic smile made Maigret realize that Naud had understood, perhaps better than might have been supposed.

"You're a first-rate person, Superintendent. . . . You really are! . . . I am so grateful."

"You'll be grateful for the rest of your

days, as a friend of mine used to say. . . . Good-by! . . . Send me a postcard from time to time."

He left the lights of the house, which now seemed stilled, behind him. Smoke rose from two or three chimneys in the village, only to disappear into the fog. The dairy was working at full capacity and, from a distance, looked like a factory. Meanwhile, old Désiré was steering his boat, laden with pitchers of milk, along the canal.

Madame Retailleau would probably be asleep by now, and the tiny postmistress, too. . . . Josaphat would be sleeping off his wine, and . . .

Right up to the last minute, Maigret was afraid he would bump into Louis. The young man had put so much faith in him and, on discovering that the Superintendent had left, would doubtless think bitterly:

"He was one of them, too!"

Or else:

"They got the better of him!"

If they *had* got the better of him, they hadn't done so with money or fine words, at any rate.

And as he stood at the end of the platform waiting for the train, and keeping an eye on his suitcase, he mumbled to himself:

"Look here, son, I, too, wish everything could be clean and beautiful, just as you do. I, too, get upset and angry when . . . ."

Surprise, surprise! Cavre walked onto the platform, stopping some fifty yards away from the Superintendent.

"That fellow, there, for instance . . . He's a crook. He is capable of all sorts of dirty tricks. I know this for a fact. And yet I feel rather sorry for him. I've worked with him. I know what he amounts to and what he suffers. . . . What would have been the point of having Etienne Naud condemned? And would they have found him guilty, anyway? . . . There is no real evidence. . . . The whole case would have stirred up a lot of dirt. Geneviève would have been called to the witness box. And Alban would have gone scot-free, probably delighted to be rid of his responsibilities."

There was no sign of Louis, which was just as well, for in spite of everything, Maigret was not proud of himself. This early-morning departure smacked too much of an escape.

"Later on you will understand. . . ."

They *are* strong, as you say. They stick together."

Having noticed Maigret, Justin Cavre came over but did not dare open a conversation.

"Do you hear, Cavre? I've been talking to myself, like a lonely old man."

"Have you any news?"

"What sort of news? The girl is all right now. The father and mother . . . I don't like you, Cavre. I am sorry for you, but I don't like you. . . . It can't be helped. Some people you warm up to and others you don't. . . . But I am going to tell you something. There is one phrase of popular wisdom that I thoroughly detest. It makes me wince and grind my teeth whenever I hear it. . . . Do you know what it is?"

"No."

"Everything will turn out all right."

The train came into the station, and in the growing din Maigret shouted:

"And you will see; everything *will* come out all right!"

Two years later, in fact, Maigret learned by chance that Alban Groult-Cotelle had married Mademoiselle Geneviève Naud in Argentina, where her father had built up a huge cattle ranch.

"Tough luck for our friend Albert, don't you think, Louis? But some poor devil always has to be the scapegoat!"

*Saint-Mesmin-le-Vieux*
*March 3, 1943*

The publishers hope that this
Large Print Book has brought
you pleasurable reading.
Each title is designed to make
the text as easy to see as possible.
G. K. Hall Large Print Books
are available from your library and
your local bookstore. Or, you can
receive information by mail on
upcoming and current Large Print Books
and order directly from the publishers.
Just send your name and address to:

G. K. Hall & Co.
70 Lincoln Street
Boston, Mass. 02111

or call, toll-free:

1–800–343–2806

*A note on the text*
Large print edition designed by
Kipling West.
Composed in 16 pt Plantin
on a Mergenthaler Linotron 202
by Modern Graphics, Inc.

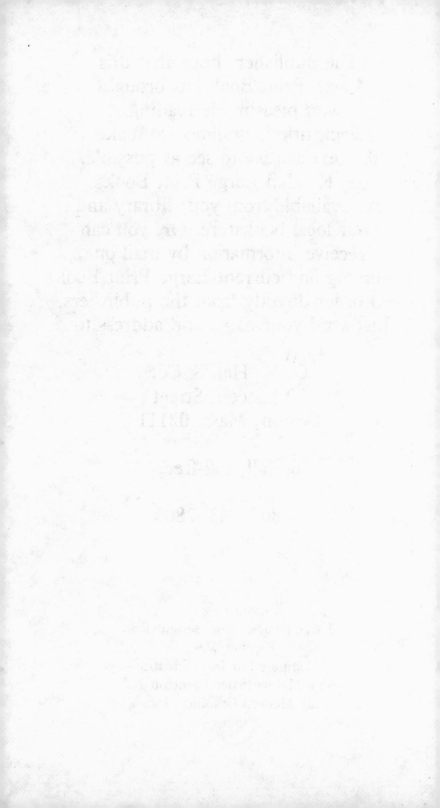